CONFERENCE OF THE CROWS

Poems by
Francis Opila

Cover Collage, Design
& Layout by Dale Champlin

Edited by Ann Farley
Author photo by Lane Cobiskey

Published by
Just a Lark Books
308 SE Walnut Street

JUST A LARK BOOKS
Hillsboro, Oregon

Body copy set in Garamond Pro

First edition

10 9 8 7 6 5 4 3 2 1

ISBN 9798890345516

for

Chris

Table of Contents

BEYOND WINGS

Shadow and Light

Roll On Columbia

Oregon Song

Beyond Wings

Conference of the Crows

As dusk settles over the urban canopy
we gather in that lively old oak,
all my aunts, uncles, nieces, nephews,
the grandbirds, hundreds of us.
Do you ever wonder
what it is we *caw* about?

Conversation a bit raucous and bold
all about the day's travels:
the views, mountain peaks, snow fields,
plow fields, urban sprawl, wetlands,
mobbing that horrid hawk on the forest fringe,
playing chicken in the road—
you should've seen my brother.
Sky fight between eagle and osprey
and how *I got the fish*.

All the gory guts, scrumptious carrion,
dumpster diving for McDonald's fries,
cheese puffs on the roadway, pizza crust,
that watermelon, spittin' out them seeds,
raided the squirrel's nut cache, did you?
—that's where I'm flyin' in the morn.
Where did you get that foul cigar butt?

O grace for Cawie's broken wing—
she may not carry on, but we love her so.
Who's willing to sit with her tomorrow?
Yes, many!
Her soul dwells in us all.

How do you pray in a murder of crows?
Sometimes it's call and response
Sometimes we wail with heartache
Sometimes we follow the woodpecker's drum
Sometimes we bow our heads.

Ah, feel the breeze!
My glossy violet-black *quivers*
with desire for my celestial
black mate, our fling of spring last,
our nest high in the great cedar.

As the moon rises, we settle,
we preen each other, snuggle
on the branches of that old oak.
We watch as owl begins her night
mission. They say she is wise,
but she's no match.

Our great, great grandbird tells a bedtime story:
A long, long time ago
when Crows were white and men were few,
wild animals reigned over the Earth.
Hunting was harsh. Then a great storm arose—
lightening leapt, vast fire surged,
smoke turned Crows black,
rain blessed the Northwest.
Great Bear descended from the stars
and gifted Crows their magic.
Men multiplied, foraging became easy,
And so it was.

And so we drift into the dream world
our roost for the night, that ancient oak.
You may wonder:
How does one rebel in a murder of crows?
Hell if I know.

Listen to Whoever Flies or Sings

Among the sage & bunchgrass,
I spot the meadowlark, radiant
yellow & black, now holding

court on a boulder, chiming his
love song, whistles & warbles
open the whole sky. I step over

paintbrush & sage, over rattlers too
cold to move, over ant hills & black
beetles, over wind & rooted

streaks of sun. I join my bird
in song, duet becoming trio,
notes of the reed flute, deep

bass of basalt cliff & wind, flare
of the river's rapids, into chorus,
into verse. It occurs to me

that I am human and my
meadowlark is a bird who flies
up the basalt outcrop, my heart

taken, but only for a moment. I look
up canyon to wind stroked ridge,
where I can soar or at least crawl.

Moth on the Sunshine Coast, BC

The bronze spots on your wings
camouflage in knots of pine,
the dark walls of the cabin.
You are hidden from light and passion.
Knowing your hunger,
I wait for you to leave
but watch only your stillness.

Finally I guide you with bare hands
toward the open window,
grasp your delicate wings,
so gently, yet clouds of moth dust
scatter on the wooden sill.
You flutter into the black night,
drawn to the silver moon
who steals behind a veil of clouds.

In the morning I wake early.
You are no longer here,
off somewhere in the frigid forest,
Arbutus and Western redcedar,
winds of emerald and moss,
grey clouds enfold beyond.
I open the screen to look for you,
but only the gold dust
of your wings remains,
spilled like incense in a shrine.

I come to talk with the Bristlecone Pines
(Pinus longaeva)

I have questions to ask
about belief, longevity,
passage. I find myself
walking among ancient trees,
over 3000 years old,
straggling foxtail branches,
shouldered by naked trunks,
stunted, gnarled, twisted,
bare rufous wood.

The sparse forest
crosses mountain side,
etches treeline,
jagged quartzite rock,
deep azure sky,
resilience beyond my miles.

I sit on a boulder,
feel the same wind the pines know.
I can't stay long at 10,000 feet,
bite of the ripping wind,
first flurries of autumn.

I voice my questions to the pines.
We talk until dusk.
Three ravens depart over the far ridge,
waxing half-moon rises in the east.
An elder whispers in the wind:
Go slow.
Feel the strength of your roots.

I take a long, deep breath,
take in the thin air, breathe again,
feel the rhythm of my heart,
start the trek down the mountain,
one foot,
then the next.

Beyond Wings

You don't ask why
a thousand geese flew over,
not twenty feet above you,
calling, cackling in the wind,
their wings beating to a drum
only you could hear.

You saw the eagle
who flushed them
from the marsh,
you saw the glint of sun
off the water, off their wings,
but you've never seen
their summer grounds.

They come over you in waves
that wash away your thoughts,
loosen your sails.
You search the blueness
beyond their wings,
beyond their Arctic lines,
circles coming home,
year after year.

When Do Crickets Stop Singing?

I wait up listening.
Reposed, my bedroll on firm ground,
dry grass, meadow at the wooded edge,
bigleaf maples, elderberry,
Oregon grape and salal.
Sizzling summer heat abates,
dew descends at twilight.

I welcome the chirping,
chant of forest and shrubs,
rhythm of bush drums,
the ebb and rippling.
I match my breath to their cadence:
seven chirps on the inhale,
seven on the exhale.

Their crescendo rises to the moon
on its zenith, serenades
the late summer stars.
A great-horned owl swoops
in hidden silence.

When do the crickets stop singing?
I rest in blackness, sip
the everlasting refrain. I remember
my last breath before dreaming:
seven chirps, seven chirps.

I awake to gentle breeze
on my face, dawn light
sprinkling on snowberries,
chorus of song sparrows.

If People Were All Trees

I wish people were all trees
and I think I could enjoy them then.
—Georgia O'Keefe 1921

You laugh gently in the breeze,
your white puffs float by, I wander
amid your clan of black cottonwoods
along the meandering river. I stop
and listen to your kin.

Mountain aspens in autumn sing
bright yellow ballads of generations gone.
Moss-covered bigleaf maples spread
winged seeds on windy afternoons.
Piñon pines bestow nuts to jays,
shrubs of the high desert,
gods of the mesa sun.
Ancient redwoods, dressed in gnarled
bark, reach for blue above the pacific mist.

I could perform this dance
with a thousand living trees
in a thousand wild worlds.

What tree would I be if I joined this family?
Would I stay where I was planted?
Would I endure the thirst of drought
and the singe of fire?
What love would my roots touch?
What songs would the wind play
in the hollows of my old age?

Maybe this river will gather
all our broken branches,
carry us to the great ocean,
where scrubbed by salt tides and sea kelp,
I could taste all these worlds.

Dragonfly Dance

Wrestle out of your shell
into morning summer light.
Stretch two pairs of wings,
open to the flow of wind,
flaunt your iridescent blue,
let sun shimmer through
your translucent wings.

Cruise across ponds,
hover over cattails,
visit sedges, devour
gnats and mayflies,
secure your territory.
Seek your mate. Embrace
your fleeting weeks
of erotic wanderings.

Somehow you know
being in a hurry
will not take you there.

Trust blue sky, long days,
afternoon heat. Hover
religiously, be present
when you meet her,
perform your coupled
dance, enmesh yourselves,
conceive the next genesis.
Know you will have copious
encounters, buzzing songs.

Know they won't last.

Statue of St. Francis in the Garden

I thought I saw you wink.

Again you wink. Then, through wild roses,
your smile reaches me. Layers of moss
peel from your concrete skin, revealing
your tattered brown cloak. You emerge

from sword ferns onto the courtyard. You say
let's have tea, so I put a pot on. Here's a chair,
a cup of green dragon tea, some biscuits. The stone
Buddha joins us with his quiet presence. I ask

Did you mind being molded from concrete or would
you have preferred being sculpted from stone?
What are your plans after all these centuries?
Do you want to hear how I've survived my hurt?
Have you heard about the latest "holy" wars?
Did you know that the pope took your name?

You simply smile and take another sip of tea.
You speak about the present moment.
A spotted towhee flits about your feet.
A fox squirrel approaches, a thief
I've come to loathe, you offer
him a few large crumbs, which he devours.

We sit. Time drifts. White petals shimmer.
We chant Brother Sun, Sister Moon.
We recite Rumi, we whirl. The wind
plays the reeds. A song sparrow trills.

I know you'll be going downtown to visit the homeless,
maybe you'll see the sisters of the road. Your path
to Assisi is long and your peace mission with the sultan
is pressing. Yet, my dear Francis, can you take some time
to walk with me barefoot in the cedar forest
and watch the trillium bloom?

Splashes of Early Summer

listen to splashes of wildflowers
oceans of prairies
songs of petals & children

hands dripping watercolors.
show us the path through
a thousand shades of green

softly blurred by wind
by desire, by opening to
early summer blooms

of crimson, canary yellow,
rose, daisies, bluebells.
bumble bees sip nectar

language pours onto canvas
into streams that carry
our voices home.

The Tree Beyond the Trees

Wildfire haze drifts gray over your sky
clearcut, burnt, dying, taken—

A new beginning
you didn't ask for.

Deep rain drenches the embers,
cleanses your breath.

Your path opens
to the tree beyond the trees,

the forest beyond the mountains,
remnant old-growth, lost

survivors. Tapestries of green
moss cloak broken limbs

and breath of lichen. Glacial
melt colors the river milk

green. A water ouzel darts
into the flow. Listen to the rapids.

Let underground streams
quench your thirst. You learn

to surrender to the color
of light.

Buddha River of Source

Awaken to the light
   of ten thousand Buddhas
   who descend the river canyon
   of a million sword ferns.

Buddhas made of earth clay
   mountain stone
   towering cedars
   fire and river flow.

Worn by water and wind
   drenched in impermanence.

Become a Buddha
   flow without effort
   among ten thousand braided
   streams.

Resist.
   Be the one who
   rages in thundering rapids
   cares little for teachings
   lusts for passion.

Allow Buddha
   to wander among wildflowers
   soar with golden eagles
   swim with spawning salmon
   bounce gently off rocks
   chant what the river chants
   pray with the saints
   sit with ten thousand Buddhas.

Subsist in silence.

River Runs Wild

What once was your river is now hers.
She emerges from mountain snows
  melting, dripping, cascading through
    your wilderness your longing
    she rattles rocks wakes your gods rips
   trees off the banks   rolls boulders
bigger than your dreams   tears at rip-rap
   and concrete dams
         spews giant logs churns
   glacial strife her banks
    sway like hips in dance she pivots
  swerves   cuts across the oxbow
  seeks beyond the floodplain
finally letting go

she lays herself out
  over your roost
  sowing sand on
reluctant
   land.

As time passes
  you no longer see her rage.
You only feel the sun glisten,
reflect off the shimmer of her skin.
Listen
  as a sweeper log drapes
  cedar boughs over gentle eddies.
Hear the trill of the kingfisher.
Grasp for what the great blue
  heron muses on a salient boulder.
Sway with the bobbing of the dipper.
Fly with mergansers arrowing
upstream, their bills burning red.
  Forgive any meanderings.
Open to the river's flow,
  be ready to dive
    when she touches you.

To Pray Under Willow Branches

rooted on Earth
river runs and you sip
its tears below ground
gather long branches
willow flex and splay
blanket over woven world
dance in black shadows
ravens chortle, soar, and dive
sky-high cottonwoods
fire flares and rocks quiver
you sweat, pray, sing
offer sufferings and thanks
dream visions of beyond
sweat onto firm ground
dive into cold river

Across the River

You dwell among clouds high across the river
Bald eagle glides in blue sky across the river

You descend from mountains, drift downstream
Show me wildflowers you sanctify across the river

You sing sans harmony on the other bank
Lost without you, I await your reply across the river

Salmon run up the riffles, bears chase and grab
What do you personify across the river?

We sailed the great ocean together,
capsized, did you die across the river?

Rapids roll and whitewater churns, I dip
my toes in, don't dare try to cross the river

Fog drips in, I hear your plaintive call
At nightfall what's your alibi across the river?

Listen to the *weet* calls of the sandpiper
You bob rock to rock by and by across the river

Asleep under cottonwoods I dream of you
On awakening you ask why? across the river

Ospreys call, ravens soar, discourse in the wind
What do words signify across the river?

The frozen river shivers in solid prose
My muse hums a lullaby across the river

My beloved sleeps in moss on the distant shore
I dive in, absorb truths, fly across the river

After You Left

I hear only the cooing moans
of the mourning dove.
My marrow cries in the black night
until morning turns pale gold.
Is the window rattling?
Is the wind praying?
I feel your warmth enter the room
You tell me you're free—
free of those old bones.
We fly, in the way that spirits fly,
to your sacred place in the woods.
We amble there for timeless moments,
for hours, maybe months.
A white hawk flies over us—
you are gone.

Sometimes I Visit the River

Sometimes I wish the road
would go on forever,
that I won't meet anyone
who wants to talk,
that when I finally reach
the river, I have it
all to myself—
rapids warble
osprey dives
kingfisher rattles
steelhead leaps.

I stay watching the night drift
across the canyon, a lone
coyote sings to his distant
cousins, sings to the distant
moon, I sing to distant stars,
letting my questions linger
unanswered, trusting only
the new dawn light.

Dry Lake

Dust devils swirl on fractured salt flats.
We search the empty expanse
for dinosaur bones, arrow heads,
shards of clay pots, petrified wood,

fossils from ancient oceans, signs
of gods and goddesses. In your thirst
for fullness, you howl to the wilds,
no reply, no echo off distant mountains.

No water source, no birds, no direction.
We taste sand in our mouths, dust
in our eyes. The wind calms at twilight.
The desert lake opens in golden hues.

Thunderheads huddle in the distant west.
We feel your breath, hushed in the cool,
still air. We lie on sun-warmed sand,
watch the Milky Way begin its dance.

White Mountain

Take yourself to Pahto[1],
the white mountain,
your vision consumed
by glaciers and white snow,
layers of conifers and stone.

Listen, breathe, find
yourself on the exposed peak,
grounded in the strength
of inner mountain.
No wind can take you
from this place.

You rise and turn, become
a whirling dervish,
every cell opens
to cloudless sky.
Spin a lunar turn,

receive what Pahto gives
what the crescent moon
and reaching stars offer.
Evolve high and wide
continuously dissolve
into indigo emptiness.

[1] *Pahto* is a name used by some Native American tribes for Mt. Adams.

Requiem for a Forest

My feet on raven earth,
smoldering ash, embers.
Scorched trees stand skeletal,
ebony, naked before lavender
sky, their crowns cremated.
Wind stirs the smoke plume,
any direction I take

the path is lost,
confused bees zigzag,
the world given to fever,
to climate forsaken
by excess and ignorance.
Yet the moon rises

full again and again,
meteors sing in dark skies.
I live by bare breaths,
my sweat drips on black
ground, seeds soak,
nutrients rebirth

fireweed, lupine, wild rose,
fungi, beetles, thrushes.
Beyond my time
pines, cedars, firs rise,
owls swoop and dive.

Metamorphosis

How easily I shed this skin
        and let the tide
        carry me out
drowning with every
        wave and surge,
        any desire expelled

I rest in buoyant swells
        cold water upwellings
descend deep hidden valleys
        among dormant volcanoes,
        fallen ancestral trees

Let me drift, wither and decay
        steep like seasoned tea
open like mycelia ripening
        disperse like spores
        in ocean streams

Shadow and Light

The Weaver Who Dyes

for D. Joel Weber

You emerge from roots, berries, bark,
grasp mounds of black walnut earth,

saffron rags and wool. Your indigo
thoughts merge, form circles

of roving around river stone.
You enter the stream of your loom:

hand deftly pitches shuttle to hand,
grip the beater and pull it hard,

batten your rug, grab the shuttle, again
and again, like tides ebbing and flooding,

tides stained indigo, lichen green, iron,
leave traces of oceans, mountains, prairies

on your hands, on your life,
salted, worn, like the fisher's hands

that work the nets, hands that wear
and never wear out. Your vision

opens a horizon of ochre suns. You
exhale seascapes, squander nothing.

Eloping

I won't be wearing a tie anymore.

We leave that night
as the wind starts,
I guide our blue canoe
like a true arrow across
that great lake, reaching
far into the wildwood.
A water flask, loaf of rye,
ninety dollars, some elk jerky,
a red rose in your flaming hair,
your sweet sweat, radiant
curves. A distant loon wails,
tremolo and grace.
Lightning cracks

in the black west sky, wolves
howl at the silver moon,
wind gusts raise fury, waves
leap, our spruce paddles dig
deep, icy spray anoints the bow,
wet chill soaks your toes.
I stop paddling—

My flute sings for you
a hymn from Venus,
I crave your heat.
I wonder if you can swim.

The Picnic

Six old Polish women wear babushkas,
walk slowly past fallow fields,
carry woven baskets,
bouquets of tulips, yellow and scarlet.
The path opens onto a sedge meadow,
blackbirds peck at dandelions,
ants crawl religiously over stones.
It's Sunday—there are no chores,
the duty of Mass is already done.
They find their place in the afternoon sun,
unfurl plaid wool blankets,
lay out flowers and food,
settle aching bones on hard ground
with no complaint.
They say grace, callused hands
folded at their waists,
they partake of bread, sausage,
bits of cheese. Talk comes in spurts,
between grass-blown silence,
thoughts about their fallen men,
about whom they dare not speak.
The matriarch opens a bottle of red wine,
six cups raise to toast, but don't touch.
The youngest starts to hum, but stops—
gusts of wind rise,
quivering day turns to dusk,
they gather their belongings,
fold the plaid blankets.
Tulip petals, yellow and scarlet,
fall to the ground.

Alaska 1983

Kodachromes of brown bears at Katmai. Picked up some walrus tusk earrings for my sweetheart. We got our oil money—bummer, it's a lot less than last year.

Good to get back out into the bush. We've been fishing the Yukon out of Emmonak. The kings are running, though not as full as last year. Still you can catch a lot in the 24 hours they give you. We've been eating salmon poached for lunch, grilled for dinner. Cleanse every night in the sweat.

It's a hard living here. The locals throw their trash in the river, can't bury it in permafrost. At the cemetery skeletons rise up from shallow graves, children who died from some white man disease. Broken outboards are scattered about, Alaskan huskies chained in teams, landlocked boats, snow machines waiting for winter storms.

We stop over in St. Mary's. A drunk staggers through the mud. The children ask me if I'm their new teacher. Back in Emmonak, we motor out in the skiff, beyond the mouth, into the Bering Sea. You can see for miles, miles of nothing but pale silver water, gray clouds. The Soviets are across there.

They shot down Korean Air passenger flight 007, spying over Soviet airspace they claimed. Killed two hundred and sixty-nine. Heard about it on the Christian radio station in Nome, the only station we get. Today it's calm here. Three ravens cavort on the wind, weaving through willows. Today you can breathe all the air you want.

Weight of the World
February 2022

I awake to the weight of the world.
Barbarity has invaded Ukraine
under smoke screens of bluster
and fire, juggernaut of
            death.

Consider a white bird bone
I found some time ago.
Maybe in the backyard?
the wetlands or forest? The bone,
as long as a postcard *(of sunflowers)*
is polished, so thin, so light,
maybe a femur or tibia
or a radius in a wing. Sometimes

I want to break it to see how strong
it is. Today already has enough
destruction. What species

is this? It's not a small bird, not a
ground bird like chicken or quail.
Perhaps a wading bird? An owl? A crane?
A bird designed to fly. And what species
am I? The same species that invaded
Ukraine? My bones are heavy,

too heavy. Show me, departed bird,
how to fly. Let me glide in today's
blue sky, let the wind carry me,
let thermals lift me to a place of
            lightness.

The Priest on the Bus

The bus putters across the aging steel bridge.
The priest, two weeks older than the pope,
wears no starched white collar,
sits every day in the same seat.
The morning fog rises off the river, exposing
the haze of my youth, the belabored
catechisms, the unspoken sins of being.
The smell of strong coffee on his breath,
he asks *How's your girlfriend?*
The current eddies under the rusted bridge.
I ask *How's that book you're writing?*

This morning the tide's flowing out.
I offer the priest a thin book of poetry,
Mary Oliver's *Thirst*, where she walks with us
to the pond, sunflowers, hummingbirds,
seekers of sweetness, but he has too
much to read. I tell him it takes two minutes

to read a poem, a randomly chosen poem,
wherever the book opens. Today he accepts
the book, opens to reflection on the ride,
opens to the next day's Mass, even in Advent,
purple vestments, shimmering candles,
his sermon offers a poem—

The fox in the field,
the yellow chat singing,
the heron in the pond,
humble prayers
of truth stirring in the ripples.

I Light a Candle for You

Well before waking of dawn
the slanting day starts with birdsong,
I light a candle lost in deep shadow.

Sunlight spills through gray clouds
to black earth. In gentle rain
I walk under sparse cedars, become

the empty path, listen to rise and fall
of day and night, melting songs
of distant warming glaciers, water surges

over jetties, floodplains. I hear cries
of many stricken by feral disease,
by racial assault, reason devoured

by lost lives, lost homes, broken streets,
finally compassion, multitudes walk
in solidarity, breathe for those who

no longer can, let me hear you sing
your purpose, your justice, your thirst.
I light a candle that shimmers at nightfall.

Remembering the Lake

Birch trees along the beach,
echo of light off white bark,
peeling of ivory scrolls,
rapping of sapsuckers & flickers,
chill wind off the lake,
golden yellow of autumn,
black night sky, stars touching
water. I don't remember

who died first. Was it the trees
or my mother? What befell
the living? Was it boring beetles
or fungus rot? Cells growing
out of control? Changing
climate? I remember

our hikes on Sleeping Bear dunes,
how we sat in the sparse shade of the
birches, branches dry and missing.
It was there you read *The Color Purple*.
Our talks on the grey-weathered
wood dock, bonfires on the beach,
your last swim out to the raft.

Making Mountains out of Molehills

Let me tout his praises:
aerating the soil, turning the earth, controlling
those bug pests. Yes, Townsend's Mole,
North America's largest. I found one
sometime ago, in my window-well, his snout
and feet naked, his rotund being covered with velvety
black fur as luscious as a black bear's. I thought
my cat might want a treat, but I took
pity on that rodent and my shovel gently guided him
to dirt where he swam away in three seconds.

Just when I was touting his praises, just then
he arrived in my yard and had a field day which
turned into a field week which lasted all summer,
making those proverbial molehills. I tried not
to be angry, who could be angry at such a beautiful,
ugly creature who primarily eats worms and bugs,
who only supplements his diet with
the succulent vegetable roots of my garden.

Alas, I shoveled off the dirt, I stamped on the
ridges above his tunnels, I cussed, but only
under my breath, since I was outwardly
touting his praises and figured I was above my
neighbor who tried to spear his little ass
with a sharp saber. One night, was it a dream?
I found myself outside with a borrowed shotgun,
oblivious to the grace of the summer moon, waiting
to unload one deadly blow on that dreaded vermin.
Thank god for time, for time is what it took to
let this damned furry beast ride off into the sunset.
Or was it the winter rains?

Even the Mice Celebrate

To scurry about the garage
        among crazy cracks and crevices
To secure a random seed
        or scrap of mulch
To make merry with kin
        in the black of night
To be safe from coyotes
        and wind howling outside
It's only when the door is left open
        and the black cat comes in
Where to hide?
        scamper to your nook
Beware when the cat is forgotten
        and the door shuts
To whisper silently—
        the party's called off.

My Garden in August

My garden sings alive in morning before red sun hits the thimble berries, the squawking of scrub jays reaches its crescendo, drowning out even the song sparrow who arrived too late, not to mention house finches lost in their own red world, while warm waves rise and dew seeks higher air, we all get our chance,

open like the golden sunflowers, who stand back behind the tomatoes, red cherries and orange slicers, who soak in every drop of light, while nearby the Italian greens, now bitter, having bolted to four feet, bear purple aster-like flowers, live among unweeded vagrants.

Across the yard the vine maple presides, in fact she flaunts the bird feeder, the likely cause of all this commotion, as shaded bleeding hearts dip their flower beings toward the living earth, full of worms and moles, who give homage under the shadow of the snowberry, its shrubness teaming

with a dozen species of bees and other pollinators, most notably the rufous humming bird, buzzing in the summer air, who will no longer be with us in winter, when all that's left for the thrushes to eat are these very same snowberries, when the cold rain gives Shiva another season.

Day of Two Suns

My breath visible in icy air, the piercing east wind blows through
the dark forest, bite of cold stings my bundled face and feet, until I
arrive at the sandy beach along the river edge, where the wind

slows, where two glaring suns perch, one low in the sky, the second
directly below, shimmering on the water surface amid ripples and
eddies. Reflection of form, energy, heat, I dare not look

at such brightness, only listen to the warble of the river, trills of
the kingfisher, warmth in my bones, stirring of my blood, quiet
of lavender sky. Time asks me

where I think I am going. I have no answer, no tangible reply, I'm
only listening. Notes of breeze-blown willows ascend, dissolve in
the quivering sky, harmonies of wind

sing in the forest canopy, overtones of flight, an eagle appears,
soaring on what may be the last thermal of the year. The afternoon
wears on, the two suns

merge on the river surface, wind-blown undulations entice the light
to dance, flare, flicker, before the fire goes out, the night upon us,
the crescent moon appears light years away.

Lord God Bird

Ivory-billed Woodpecker *(Campephilus principalis)*

—Kenn Kaufman, Audubon.org, May 29, 2020

To be the Lord God Bird
>	ghost of bottomland forests,
>	sweet gums and cypress, Atchafalaya
>	bayous, cathedrals, unspoken
>	backwaters and swamps, panthers
>		and cottonmouth snakes.

You know me by my immense being—
>	greater than my Pileated cousin—
>	by my ivory bill, red crest,
>		unwavering flight,
>	double-rap
>		on old-growth snags.

You know me, but you've never seen me.
>	You search the Big Woods of Arkansas,
>		bald cypress swamps, canopy
>		and sunshine.
Phantom fires rage, my wings singed
>		and black—

I sing the wind blowing upstream,
>	flare the quake of earth across time,
>		glide in vanishing dark forests.

Someone, somewhere saw me sail
            among extinct Passenger Pigeons.
Now I am the call of the Mourning Dove.

Tis the Season

As if I could avoid another holiday.
Wind came and with great breath
blew the tops of trees. Evergreen pinnacles
swayed and whirled like devout dervishes.
Ready branches came free and joined
duff on the forest floor, where I found one
with a sweet curve, an offering from
a Douglas fir, a swag on the door. My beloved
tied a red ribbon on it. We called it Christmas.

Vignettes of Winter

1

Afternoon light has nothing
not even the bare-naked trees.
Dimness of sleep descends
like winter fog, frozen in a window
of time. You light a candle that
sings your love for me.

2

East wind whips out of the gorge,
shifting sunlight steals your shadow.
You are gone. Was it wind or flight?
A flock of bushtits sails in,
flicker and chirp in lonely trees
vanish in crimson sun.

3

Nothing moves, yellow foliose lichen
on fallen boughs, withered brown
leaves on umber ground, only
the chilled rhythm of whiteness,
flurries ease toward earth.
Stillness is all I hear.

4

Thunder snow shrouds the land,
floats down so lightly, a veil
of nothingness. I am quilted
in powder dreams.

5

My dream: I light your candle, feel
again your flame, we melt,
lie together on sunlit ivory sand
tropical waves gently roll over us
whales spout offshore.

6

My eyes open in white,
the world is somewhere
in a hurry, its laughter muffled
by snow, I'm lost to all
but the beat of my heart.

7

A skein of tundra swans descends over
the frozen marsh, necks straight
as arrows. The river, ice free, sweeps
out bend after bend. A hooded merganser
dives into that cold, never to reappear
in that watercolor scene.

8

There is no lull as rain pelts down
in puddles of gray, white turns
to ash, ice to slush, glisten to
shadow, walking to wading.

9

Balmy blue and gray, pale sun,
thorns of wild rose, broken branches
all thaw, soften. Songbirds flit
in leafless shrubs, *chickadee-dee-dee*.
I hear your melody, your sweet fragrance
drifts under the crescent moon
of evening. Where are you?

Uprooted

When your song is taken away
and gray clouds hover low,
hummingbirds whisper
your name—christened in
magenta blossoms of
salmonberry. The river fills

with your tears, carries
your dreams downstream.
Onshore cedar and maple
exhale healing breeze. High up
in cottonwoods bald eagles
call *klee-kee-kee*, their nest
hatches new life. You migrate

in blue sky, take only
what your wings carry,
your return uncertain.
The wind blows still.
You cry for home.

A Pair of Cedar Waxwings Drops By

We haven't seen them for over a year. They flit about the branches of the hawthorn and sample the not-yet-ripe berries.

But they really came here to see you. I can't bear to tell them that you are gone, that you are on a journey, a pilgrimage through a deep canyon.

Their rakish black masks hide their eyes. They flash their canary-yellow tail tips, hoping you will show yourself. They raise their shiny chestnut crests, probe the breeze, whistle high-pitched calls that sound like sighs.

I tell them to come back when the berries are plump and purple, when our world is ready for whatever flies here.

Three Crows at the Lake
Sleeping Bear Dunes, Michigan

They come by every morning, comb the beach, cruise the forest canopy, cawing raucously to the world. I finally realize that they are calling us, urging us

into the summer day, not with the sweetness of the cardinal's song, nor the openness of the breeze gracing the leaves, but calling us before we can make any plans. We have our coffee and tea, our placid moments before

we hike among the cedar, maples, and beech, who lead us up the steep dune, through thunder, wind gusts, rain, the sun's burn upon the sand, up the bluff of the sleeping mother bear where we look out on that immense lake, where I think I see whales, where we do see two bear cubs at rest,

their black backs breaking the water surface. We swim without fear out to the crib, where we float effortlessly in cool water, blueness, terns fish from above, the sky cradles its clouds. The fall of night gently slopes over us, the wind stops, black sky holds the stars, Ursa Major and Minor, shooting stars, the whole Milky Way, leaving the Moon

to light some other sky, some other night. We are drawn to sleep, to dream our own stories, crickets drumming, Venus revealed, before the bird songs of morning, the call of the crows.

Roll On Columbia

Roll On Columbia: An Epilogue

after Woody Guthrie's "Roll On, Columbia, Roll On"

I am morning rain
dripping off conifers
Icy glacial melt
awakens my thirst
I take a few deep breaths
let springs rise from within

My source is sourceless
My headwaters have no place of origin
Yet somewhere in the Canadian Rockies
I emerge

gather cascading streams,
plunge downward,
slice through canyon chutes,
I breathe water
I exhale water
My shorelines migrate
I change course on a whim

I no longer sit behind clay dams
I re-craft wild cataracts
Priest Rapids, *Dalles des Morts*
Forest once drowned grows feral
Salmon spawn in all my streams
my tributaries
my contributaries
my visionaries

My totems are here
Bears black and brown visit and play
Deer and Elk graze and drink abundance
Families of Otter frolic in my eddies
A pack of Wolves
unnamed unnumbered
howl moonfully from my bank
Beavers love-slap my water skin
Coyote dances on the cliff edge
Soaring Eagle blesses my winding course

I cross no boundary between nations
There is no Canada
There is no United States
My path carries around Roosevelt's dam
I roam over the Grand Coulee
I spill wetness over Dry Falls
Where once salmon were halted
I now let them walk up my arms

On the Hanford Reach
I feel radioactive shock
still cooking after all these centuries
I cough toxic sand and roll on

I meet my goddess river the Snake
She brings sweet cold water
more than I can breathe
We rejoin, we marry, we roll on

Today there are no tugs
No barges carrying gravel and grain
No merchant ships with cars and phones
No railways, bridges, or dams
No outfall pipes spewing waste
No dikes, riprap, or seawalls

Today I carry salmon smolts
on their circle of destiny
Sturgeon grow ancient in my sleep
I roll on
I hear distant drumming
I briefly linger in a pool

[*Coyote winks at me*
  I swirl a whirlpool in reply]

I drop over Celilo Falls
once smothered, now alive
I roar over craggy rocks
My breath becomes spirit spray

Clans of first peoples—
Chinook, Klickitat,
Yakama, Nez Perce,
Sk'in-a-ma, many more
gather on my shore
drum on Antelope skins
dance the Salmon song
fish the free-falling falls
taste again the Salmon power
give thanks to the Great Spirit
retell old Coyote tales

[*Coyote grins*
  scampers away]

Across my flank
in her garden of rock
She Who Watches[1] waits
Her eyes shine on river souls

The remains of dams
lie on my bed
I slowly grind concrete
into round boulders,
turbines into sleeping rust
all buried in my sandy belly

I sail through the Gorge
I recall the last great flood
some centuries ago
when I carried volcanic ash
when I ventured a new path

Bridge of the Gods resurrected
arches her beneficent back
River souls amble across
I glide under her smooth shadow
I roll on

I bask in the snow-capped radiance
of Wy'east[2] and Pahto[3]
who no longer hurl stones of fire,
their jealousy now abated
Their beloved beauty Loowit[4]
rests, liberated, her eruption spent

[1] She Who Watches is a Native American petroglyph overlooking the
Columbia River in the area of Wishram, Washington.

[2] Wy'east is a name associated with Mt. Hood. It may have been used by
the Multnomah tribe.

[3] *Pahto* is a Native American name for Mt. Adams.

[4] *Loowit* is a Native American name for Mt. St. Helens.

Thunderbird rides on thermals
soaring high on 10-foot wings
Sky jumps with fire bolts
Sun paints rainbows on slate

The once muddy Willamette
comes to me clear and cool
We swell over marshes and sloughs
Hundreds of thousands of ducks,
geese honking, swans, and cranes
ascend and fly about
The cacophony is prayer
The prayer is wildness

Ghosts of street people
come to visit my shore
They linger, camp under stars
rest in the peace of moonlight
drink my holy water
without filters or fear
They gaze at salmon running
once a lucrative catch,
now a savory dream

I rouse fluid might
I am rolling thunder
I am flowing free
The Corps no longer dredges my guts
I wash away the sand islands
built with my precious entrails
I roll on

I feel the pulse of incoming tide
I sense the magnificent Ocean
I taste salt
I don't want to mix
yet I'm propelled from beyond

I make my way onto the bar
We clash, buck, and surge
We roil whalebones and ship masts
We spit dragon spray
Then I am beyond
I dissolve in swells
There are no dead zones
I breathe, salmon breathe
I catch a current,
drift to where albatross fly
dissolve again
and again

I am morning rain
dripping off conifers
Icy glacial melt
awakens my thirst
I take a few deep breaths
let oceans rise from within.

Fate of Eighteen Dams on the Columbia River

*As of 2022, there are eighteen mainstem dams on the
Columbia River, including four dams on its main tributary,
the Snake River.*

She Who Watches has not drowned.
Treaties signed in the 1850's promised
the right to fish in usual & accustomed places.
Salmon runs decline. Migrations trickle.

Treaties signed in the 1850's promised
a way of life stolen from future generations.
Salmon runs decline. Migrations trickle
stopped by the Grand Coulee Dam.

A way of life stolen from future generations
Our paddles dip in quickening flow
stopped by the Grand Coulee Dam.
White-washed skies sweat tears

Our paddles dip in quickening flow
Did Chief Joseph want a dam named for
white-washed skies that sweat tears?
Our canoe blown by angry winds

Did Chief Joseph want a dam named for
flooded Celilo Falls and fishing grounds?
Our canoe blown by angry winds
thirteen distinct populations threatened or endangered

Flooded Celilo Falls and fishing grounds
Warming temperatures stress & kill
thirteen distinct populations threatened or endangered
We portage around resurrected rapids

Warming temperatures stress & kill
Woody Guthrie sings "Roll On, Columbia"
We portage around resurrected rapids
A century of dams unravels in days

Woody Guthrie sings "Roll On, Columbia"
Right to fish in usual & accustomed places
A century of dams unravels in days
She Who Watches smiles at salmon running.

OREGON SONG

Caldera Collage
Crater Lake, Oregon

Crystal dance of sunlight, cerulean trance, depths beyond our vision, boat cruise in morning mist. We envision the eruption of ancient Mount Mazama, collapsed into caldera. We walk the rim among windswept whitebark pines, pumice landscape splashed with wildcolor—paintbrush, penstemon, lupine. In lawn chairs on the ledge, we watch everything fall into night, black sky & Milky Way, Venus, Mars, Jupiter, we float in vastness.

Three-Legged Coyote (*Canis latrans*)
Ankeny National Wildlife Refuge, Oregon

At the edge of the winter marsh,
she prances on three legs,
front left stump dangling,

her lush tawny coat streaked
black and crimson, tail bushy,
her frame full, muscles flexed,

ears raised, she glides
among the rushes and sedges.
Her keen eyes trace the world

of mallards, shovelers,
green-winged teals, wigeons,
and buffleheads, searching

for one with broken wing
or fallen to some avian disease.
She disregards the peregrine

streaking above, the eagles
perched in the cottonwoods.
Only we see her, flicker of ear,

steam of warm breath,
glint of canines, subtle grin.
The wind turns from the north,

late afternoon sun sinks,
clouds dip in rose, she's gone,
her ghost howls in frigid fog.

Green-winged Teal (*Anas crecca*)
Sauvie Island Wildlife Area, Oregon

Late afternoon angled sun,
I watch you on the marsh—
chestnut head, dark green eyepatch,
buff rump, you struggle, your head
barely above water, the wind dies.

The hunt continues, camo garb,
willow-covered hunting blind,
retriever pointed, silent, ready,
decoys in brilliant color waft
among sedges—shotgun rings
out, reverberates across the marsh,
echoes off copses and old barns.

Your teal wing feathers shine,
floating, now far from the hunt,
no longer able to hold your head
aloft, there is no prize, no check in
with fish & wildlife, your spirit
abandoned, I still breathe.

Oregon Morning Song

Listen to waves tuned to light
absorbed by tidal clouds, mist

of morning surf, frigid
green-gray sea crashes

over sculpted rocks, flowing
sand. Your footprints wash

away, gulls cry for their morning
feast, I sing for your return.

Sand crabs scurry, pelicans drift
by blue horizons, white sun

pierces clouds, tide sweeps logs,
forests revive. The sky blows

riffs of wind and rain, your wings
sail through turbulence.

Persephone Farm

for Elanor

The sliver crescent moon sets,
awakens black emptiness,
red Mars in opposition,
Venus in the west,
Jupiter, Saturn flirt to the south,
the Summer Triangle at zenith.

I lie on my cot in the field,
gaze at the show—the Perseids,
torch companions to Polaris.
I hear meteors sing in bright codas,
I hear the clank of the distant rail yard,
crickets in full chirp.
All drift into the underworld.

Night dew soaks my blanket,
river rapids drone past the fields,
sprinkler spray tones *psst-psst-chk*,
notes of fennel waft in mist.
My eyes stir in amber light,
sky lost in gray clouds.

Persephone floats over the fields,
her dark hair flowing long,
her last act of the season.
Workers glide in fog,
don green rain pants,
slash broccoli tops,
chard, pumpkins, and squash,
hustle along the rows,
lift blue bins into the truck.

I rise, open my dream eyes,
open late to the morning breeze,
faces of sunflowers,
aroma of sodden earth,
subterranean draw,
the harvest of planets and stars.

Wapato Island

—William Clark, *Lewis and Clark Journals*
    edited by Gary E. Moulton

We hide under the old oaks.
Dusk rides over the island.
A glimmer of setting sun
reveals wings in flight.
They come in threes, fives, a dozen,
flying like arrows,
their long necks held straight
they bugle, chortle, and rattle,
their calls older than cave art.

The Sandhill Cranes cruise in
from corn fields,
shift course when they spot us,
parachute down into Sturgeon Lake
perform their primal dance,
choreographed over eons:
leaping, dipping, flapping, bowing.
They join the gathering hundreds,
a roost in the shallow marsh
where they are stained cinnamon red,
where Coyote does not venture.

Their song lifts and falls
answered by the calls of hundreds
of Canada Geese,
dozens of White-fronted,
but no Brants.
A Cessna roars over,
drowns out the avian chorus.

Ghosts of Multnomah Indians
gather here, chant with the cranes,
dig up roots of arrowleaf *wapato*.
Today they no longer dwell here—
decimated two centuries ago
by intruders' epidemic fever.

The ruby sun dips into the Coast Range.
We stay into the darkness,
the cranes sail in by the score,
thousands by now,
their crescendo pulses.

It's our last night
before the gate is locked
and hunting begins.
We walk out slowly in the dark
avoiding cow pies,
the grass nibbled to the ground.

The sliver moon rises.
We hear the deep hooting
of a Great-horned Owl,
its black shadow glides over us.
In a nearby field,
a coyote howls.

Among Lava Flows
Newberry Volcano, Oregon

Our paddles dip in the frigid water,
the blue canoe glides effortlessly
across the caldera pool
where the volcano collapsed,
we float among western grebes,
rafts of buffleheads and coots,
shoals of kokanee salmon.

We reach the shore—
pyroclastic flow, *young* lava,
young like raven fledglings,
discharged only 1300 years ago,
lava that surged over basalt
over alluvial deposits
over sediment from Missoula floods.

We met some years ago
on a nearby trail
among ponderosa pines,
the play of Clark's nutcrackers.
A flock of Oregon juncos followed us
until we wandered into the lava tube,
where in the faint glow
    we embraced.

Flows of rhyolite rock—
boulders of obsidian,
blacker than ebony,
edges of midnight silver
that cut through ice,
become arrowheads,
knives, scrapers of buckskin.

The earth shudders—
horizons quiver and spin
icy waves crash over the bow
the canoe rolls—
we brace on the gunnels
our boat rights itself,
we await shock waves,
eruption of fire and ash.

Seconds feel
        like hours. In slow motion
we paddle doggedly,
come ashore on the beach,
rolling white pumice stones.

Our feet slip-slide,
we hold each other close
        waiting—
the earth stops trembling,
sky reflects deep blue.

Western Trillium (*Trillium ovatum*)

—a perennial herb with 3 triangular oval leaves, blooms for about 3 weeks in Pacific Northwest forests, showing off its 3 large white petals.

Mystic
guest,
uncatholic
trinity.
Imbibes
morning
mist,
beloved
ether.
Sings
understory
hymns
with
wild ginger
bleeding heart
twisted stalk.
Bows
down to
cloudbursts
hail showers.
Awakens for
sun breaks.
Sparkles
up spires
cedar
hemlock
Douglas fir.

Waltzes
the Moon.
Wilts
purple,
longing
belonging
silence.

Oregon Swallowtail (*Papilio oregonius*)

I wrestle out of my chrysalis—
fattened up on tarragon sage
    deep dreams of black and yellow flight.
Open these wings wide and stretch
    flutter off into blue air.

Ride the Deschutes canyon wind
    in dips, swoops, and glides.
Follow the basalt ledge
    to bright suns of balsamroot,
    sweetness of nectar,
    thistle and phlox.

Free now to take up the chase
    I see her rising,
    breaking into her first flight
    her colors are ecstatic—
We meet on the wing
    we mate, she descends to the sage.
I ascend for another quest—
    if I live a full two weeks
    what love will the days bring?

Pumkin-eeeeater
Flash of brilliant red!
The red-winged blackbird
    dives at me
        I spin an erratic dance
        Ouch!—he caught the tip of my tail
    I drop down into brambles
    of wild rose. He's gone—
I can still fly!

My flight now in disarray
      gusts take me downstream,
      I flow with dry cottonwood leaves,
      shreds of snakeskins.
I hold on to
      distant memory of love.

High Tide Line / Unresolved

Color sings off the ocean—
sunlight plays azure,
aquamarine, surf blue
scattered by gales
shattered by storms
from across the Pacific
China, Viet Nam, the Philippines
to Oregon breakers
faded reds, yellow, blue,
veins of color, magenta, cyan,
plastic bits, kaleidoscope
of broken jugs, torn fish nets,
six-pack rings, straws, bottles,
once drinking water, Coca Cola,
Nestle, Amcor, Unilever, PepsiCo,
petroleum, now pelagic trash,
polyethylene, polypropylene,
polyvinyl chloride, polystyrene,
dumped into streams,
carried by surging rivers—
Yangtze, Mekong, Ganges,
thrown overboard off ships,
flammable, melted,
half-lives of millennia,
washed by deep rivers, sand, salt,
displacers of plankton, squid, krill,
coated with algae like bait,
swallowed by albatross,
shearwaters, petrels,
stomachs ruptured,

birds perish, starvation,
sea turtles snared,
plastic shards, fibers,
fragments, microbeads,
nanoplastic soup,
Pacific gyre escapees,
carried on swells,
pushed by waves,
pulled by tides,
out onto the sand,
Oregon north coast beach,
high tide line,
alongside rotting kelp,
plastic bits, drowned,
broken, blanched,
forever adrift.

The Willamette Stone

Willamette Stone State Heritage Site, Oregon
45.5195° N, 122.7438° W

Listen to the muffled roar of trucks
on Highway 26. Draw near
the rusted corner post adorned
with barbed wire. Look up
into cold fog—the frigid metal
cell tower competes with Douglas fir
and bigleaf maple. The ground's
covered with fir cones, withering
brown leaves, a Snickers wrapper.

* * *

In 1851 white settlers drove a red cedar
stake into wet black soil, conceived
the Willamette Meridian and Baseline.
Proclaimed Oregon Territory in rectangles:
townships, ranges, sections of 640 acres.

* * *

To survey this land
into borders and fences
bring disease and false treaties,
let your kin encroach,
block refugees from any home.

* * *

Fauna and flora heed no boundary—
English ivy creeps, chokes Oregon
grape and salal. Spiny thickets
of European holly shroud
understory buds.

* * *

May we return here someday—
ask forgiveness of Earth and clans,
welcome home the Kalapuya,
open to canopy and clear sky.
Leave the stone itself, geodetic
marker forgotten, weathered
under the duff of decay,
vine maple and twisted stalk.

Only Oregon Rain

Birthed by tides and gales, Pacific swells outpace only rain
Our stories mix with melting snow, erase only rain

Douglas firs send rivulets onto maiden hair and sword fern
Trills of the Pacific wren rise up, interlace only rain

Deep in the wilderness—cedar, lichen, and moss
What do you unveil in this sacred place? only rain

Cascading rivers sing whitewater refrains
Spawning salmon run upstream, retrace only rain

Look out the winter window into gray morning mist
Vision wanders, nights of white frost lace only rain

What deity do you seek on this cloudy black night?
Raise your gaze to Orion, face only rain

Float the wide Columbia, behold She Who Watches
Become the swift current, race only rain

Run with pronghorn antelope across the sage steppe
Swirling dry desert winds chase only rain

Wildfires rage, ride roiling gusts, leap fleeing rivers
Who can save this desolate place? only rain

When squalls batter your soul, where is your refuge?
Hail storms percuss metal roofs, disgrace only rain

My heart breaks and tears fall, consoled by gray skies
I seep into cold streams, embrace only rain

I hike up the volcano Wy'east, trail to the Great Sky
Mountains are lost in white out, displace only rain

Along the willowed stream Francis hears the song of reeds
Sunbreaks open blue sky, rainbows grace only rain

Indian-Pipe (*Monotropa uniflora*)

Waxy white
you rise out of emerald green
like a wild orchid,
among myriads of mosses
barely touched by dampened sun.

You lack chlorophyll,
yet you're nursed
by mycorrhizal nerves,
grounded by old Douglas firs.

As if you were a ghost. As if
wolf urine begged you to life.
Wind rises from your pipes,
fills the whole forest.
You foretell an abundance
of wood mushrooms. You heal
open wounds. Rain is all
you desire. As if you thought
no one would notice.

Flute Player by the Deschutes River

after Mary Oliver's "There is a Place Beyond Ambition"

I am still there, listening.
To rapids running to their place.
To the sun rising over the ridge,
the silence of high desert rimrock,
thermals gathering waves on which
red-tailed hawks surf and cavort.

The riven columns of basalt cliffs,
rocks broken off centuries ago,
today tell stories of ice and floods,
of lives gone and now resung.

I open to the sandy earth,
black beetles, wild grass singing,
elderberries, old cottonwoods,
the broken branch, pith gone, hollow,
the river breeze sings, plays the flute,
my breath rides there
as if it were my own.

The canyon wren answers:
a descending verse of melodic beads
cascading unhurriedly to the river's flow,
where the shimmer of many moons
echoes across the water.

Balsamroot in the Columbia Basin

The night of the hard frost, the icy moon showers its cold light on the rock soil, dawn brings red-winged blackbirds singing among meadowlarks. You wonder, what song do you sing on the edge of your love, as you thaw, opening to balsamroot in bloom, their sunny faces splash gold over the sagebrush steppe, along basalt cliffs, desert parsley, prairie lupine, you know your way home, but you're still adrift, deep shadows sink on the Columbia below, wind on the edge of the precipice, turkey vultures soar on thermals and gusts.

Rattlesnake on the Owyhee Reservoir

I had never seen a rattler swim.
He races within feet of my canoe—
fear jumps in my gut.
     He swims
          away in sinuous S's
    over placid water.
Some campers spot him, yell out,
fire up their outboard, take chase
     in their skiff.

Because the men hate snakes.
They fear its bite, its venom,
     its existence.

Across the reservoir the snake
flees, climbs the vertical rock wall
     there is no ledge, no haven.
The squad catches up, pins it
with an oar, crushes its head—
blood oozes
blood crimson red
     like yours and mine,
blood weeps, stains
     the tawny rock face.

Autumn Rain Speaks

I wonder what the rain speaks
to thousands of cackling geese
who circle over all I behold.

I raise my arms to the sky, feel
yesterday's mist on my temples
my dreams flow in swelling streams

find another way to the muddy river.
The geese cackle and call, I listen
and breathe, gray clouds depart

black skies open to stars
illuminate the geese settling
to roost in the widening marsh.

Last chirps of cold chorus frogs
descend into mud clay worlds
being what the rain speaks.

Common Loon (*Gavia immer*)
Hood Canal, Olympic Peninsula, Washington

Cool gray clouds lay low in monochrome layers
The windless fjord is dappled by silver drops

Gentle autumn rain, cold rain, slack water
I taste the air, salt, decaying seaweed

Traverse the shoreline, wander among
broken oyster shells and coarse stone

Onshore bigleaf maples droop gold leaves
A few parachute to damp ground

On edges and cliffs, peeled bark of madrones
glistens wet amber and sienna

The loon glides in the offshore calm
Her winter costume drab gray and white

No regal black and white plumage, no stripes
and checkerboard like the northern lakes of summer

No tremolos and wails echo across the water
Now she dives into the deepness

Uncounted time passes, she surfaces in stillness
We dwell awhile in the fading pearl light

Winter Walk in Forest Park
Portland, OR

It's a city park, you know.
Sometimes a chance moment comes
when a dusting of snow covers
  the temple floor
when I stroll the muddy path
  and my breath wanders
when passing hikers inexplicably
  speak in hushed tones
when there are no runners or dogs
when the roar of road hum
  stays silent
when everything is still—
I hear whispers of understory talk
murmurs of sword ferns
a splash of wild ginger
bitter discord of invasive ivy

When I come upon my revered
  old-growth Douglas fir
sometimes I just look up and stare
sometimes I touch its bark with my bare hands
sometimes we share a bear hug
sometimes I want to crawl
  into its innards
  and curl up and sleep
  for a year or two

A tiny Pacific wren appears
flitting, chirping, chatting
his erect tail points to the sky
He tells me his story
     of winter
     of solitude
     of yearning—
longing to sing his cascading
     trill to his beloved
it's early though, only January
I wonder where she sleeps
It's a city park, you know.

Requiem for the Sea Star
Oregon Coast, 2014

1

What currents brought you here?
Your tenacious legs splay
steady on wave swept rocks,
your palette shines sunshine
orange, cinnamon brown, orchid
violet, among purple sea urchins
and green anemones. We drift
with you for hours, your domain
of intertidal zone, your appetite
for urchins and mussels, drinking
in all the tidal ebbs and flows.

2

What current takes you away?
Your tenuous hold loosens
in over-cooked water.
They call it *wasting syndrome*—
devoured by unseen, black plague,
you lose your arms in the abyssal
draw, fade to rotting pulp,
dusk gray, smoke, ghostly white,
dripping from jagged rocks
local extinction
we perish with you.

3

We await your resurrection
unfolding stars in the night,
the prophetic new moon.

Unfolding Leaves

Lan Su Chinese Garden, Portland, OR
November

Late sun plays on lily pads,
floating leaves pass idly
across the black pond,
paths of red and gold
fade inevitably in decay.

Shadows of the masters
amble along the bank,
limbs of shore pines splay
like moth trails in the sky.
Falling sunlight echoes
off *Tai Hu*[1] rock faces,
weaves openings in stone.

Words of truth radiate,
drift upward, not lasting
more than a few sips
of bamboo leaf tea,
yet dwell wholly
in the jewel in the lotus.

---

[1] *Tai Hu* stone was imported from Lake Tai (or Lake Taihu), a lake
in the Yangtze Delta and one of the largest freshwater lakes in China.

Caravan of Gray Whales

They come blowing geysers

breach the nomadic swell

tail flukes to the wind

full moon beckons their passage

murrelet wings chase to sea

drifting redwood fog lifts

sun carries mist off fireweed

light drips from primal beings

south passage to winter waters

graybacks dive the pacific deep

bellow in monochrome

ocean waves drink dark

Another Conversation with Sandy River

Chortles of river rush, alluvial tones of sand
& stone & silence, I sit on driftwood shore.

My river & I have spoken a thousand times.
I ask variations of questions I've been asking

for centuries. Tell me about gravity
& entropy. Where does loss go? What of

our cat's demise, saying goodbye? Why
did cancer flare in my sister, nearly

our mom's age at passing? We do not
choose our trajectory, maybe not even

what hearts we touch along the way.
We didn't conceive the lilt of bird song

among trillium & cedar in the mossy forest.
How magenta hue saturates fairy slipper

orchids under towering firs. How mergansers
fly upstream not two feet above river flow.

Today I breathe clean air & blue sky, recite
the same poem you've heard a thousand times.

The answers float, not quite discernible,
yet pacifying: a gentle breeze, balmy sun.

Violet-green swallows skim the surface,
snatch hovering flies. As the river surges

it's time to walk.

When I Go

Take my body to the Oregon desert,
maybe to Steens Mountain,
down to the Alvord,
or somewhere out
on the sagebrush steppe.

Let vultures have my flesh,
perhaps a kettle or two will drift in,
maybe a pair of ravens will join the party.
Let the wind take my ashes
in whatever direction it chooses.
Let coyotes scatter
                    my bones.

May a flock of white pelicans pass over me,
spiral skyward on desert thermals.
May my heart stay with you for a while,
perhaps for several new moons.

Look for me in the winter night—
somewhere above Orion.
Listen for my flute song,
may we all sing gentle waves
that wash wildness
                    over our Earth.

Acknowledgments

Grateful acknowledgement is made to these publications in which these poems first appeared, sometimes in different form and under different titles:

Aji Magazine: "If People Were All Trees," "Moth on the Sunshine Coast, BC"

The Avocet: "Beyond Wings"

Cirque: "Three-Legged Coyote (*Canis latrans*)"

Clackamas Literary Review: "The Picnic"

Latitude on 42nd, Empirical Magazine: "Conference of the Crows," "Trillium," "Winter Walk in Forest Park"

Parks and Points, Wayfinding: "Balsamroot in the Columbia Basin," "I Come to Talk with the Bristlecone Pines (*Pinus longaeva*)," "Caldera Collage" (originally published as "Postcard from Crater Lake")

The Poeming Pigeon: "The Weaver Who Dyes"

Soul-Lit: "Statue of St. Francis in the Garden," "The Priest on the Bus"

Willawaw Journal: "Among Lava Flows," "Wapato Island"

Windfall: "High Tide Line / Unresolved"

Multnomah Art Center poetry post selection: "Listen to Whoever Flies or Sings"

In Gratitude

To Chris for listening and always being there. For loving my work (and me) no matter what revision.

To my writing teachers (in order of appearance in my journey): Kim Stafford, Peter Sears, Sherri Levine, Christine Colasurdo, and John Morrison, for their inspiration and for pushing me to improve.

To Ann Farley for her encouragement and exquisite help in editing this collection.

To Dale Champlin, publisher, for her support and inspiring design work.

To our supportive poetry community in Portland, OR.

In Memory Of

Christine Colasurdo, with much gratitude for her artistry, writing, calligraphy, insights, her communion with nature, and for sharing it all. Several of the poems in this collection were created in Christine's class *Reading and Writing About Oregon.*

Praise for *Conference of the Crows*

In Francis Opila's debut poetry collection, *Conference of the Crows*,
he asks the reader "How do you pray in a murder of crows? / Sometimes
it's call and response / Sometimes we wail with heartache / Sometimes
we follow the woodpecker's drum / Sometimes we bow our heads."
This confounding question and many others reveal Opila's passionate
and spiritual journey of discovery and exploration. There is quiet and
exhilaration as in "Listen to Whoever Flies or Sings" and "Beyond
Wings." Most of his poems are filled with love, loss, joy, wonder, and
gratitude. His beautiful and compassionate collection ponders profound
questions and tries to provide a revelatory path toward understanding
them. He is not afraid to open his heart and invite us in.

> —Sherri Levine, author of *Stealing Flowers from the Neighbors*

Francis Opila is an adventurer, now in the mind of a crow, now in
the hunger of a three-legged coyote, now in the terror of an escaping
rattlesnake. Because of his shape-shifting, it's tempting to say his keen
attention catches everything we miss, including our larger stories of
cruelty and destruction. And yet, with a steady voice in a book that is
gentle and brave, he illuminates the world he steps into ahead of us.

> —John C. Morrison, author of *Monkey Island* and
> *Heaven of the Moment*

Conference of the Crows offers a field guide to voices rising from immersion in wild places. The poet meets and honors madrone, fir, loon, wren, rattler, balsamroot, fern, and all such cousins—all precious citizens of forest and desert, river and ocean wave. Speaking of a creature, to a creature, or in the voice of a creature, Opila's poems enter into conversation, asking, seeing, honoring the vibrant lives surrounding and sustaining the human. Whether in a city park or the Owyhee desert, Opila steps close to grow by each encounter. These are poems to companion your own forays beyond screens, wires, machines, and streets. Carry this book into the open, and savor it.

—Kim Stafford, author of *Singer Come from Afar*

Francis Opila is an astute and authentic observer of the natural world—but he does much more: he worships at its altar. Passionate and reverent about the flora and fauna that populate *Conference of the Crows,* he disdains no creature, honoring even rattlesnakes and moles. All beings and environments are opportunities for communion—for instance, the unassuming moth: "…only the gold dust / of your wings remains, / spilled like incense in a shrine." An epic six-page poem, "Roll On Columbia: An Epilogue," inspired by the centerpiece of Woody Guthrie's Columbia River songs, is especially compelling. All the poems in *Conference…* are engaging, informative and inspiring, even those that address destruction of the environment. Authoritative yet humble, Opila's clear and compassionate poetic voice deserves to be heard.

—Leah Stenson, author of *Life Revised* and
editor of *Reverberations from Fukushima:
50 Japanese Poets Speak Out*

Francis Opila—Bio

Francis Opila is a rain-struck, sun-loving poet who lives in
the Pacific Northwest. His work, recreation, and spirit have
taken him into the woods, wetlands, rivers, mountains, and
deserts. As a young man, Opila shunned poetry after enduring
uninspiring lessons as a student. Some years ago, he discovered
Rumi, which opened to a profusion of other poets, which led
to now. *Conference of the Crows* is his debut collection of poetry,
a compilation of poems from a dozen years through 2023. He
enjoys performing poetry, combining recitation and playing
North American wooden flutes.